Careerpreneur KickStart

25 Ways to Subtract Fear and Add Success To Your Business!

By Naketa R. Thigpen

- Fulfilled Clinician, Barrier Breaking Businesswoman & Careerpreneur

Guiding Women from *Idle to Awesome*

Careerpreneur KickStart

Copyright © 2014 by Naketa R. Thigpen

All rights reserved. No part of this book may be reproduced or transmitted in any form or by any means without written permission of the author.

Table of Contents

Introduction 1

Chapter 1 Stages of Growth 4

Chapter 2 Picking Your POM POM's 5

Chapter 3 First Fruits Prioritization 8

Chapter 4 General Office Hours 9

Chapter 5 Specialized Office Hours 11

Chapter 6 Relationship Management 13

Chapter 7 Harvest Time 16

Chapter 8 Designer Tassels 18

Chapter 9 Spark It Up! 20

Appendix I: POM POM Complete 29

Appendix II: POM POM Mind Map 30

About The Author 31

About The Company 33

Introduction

Are you a Careerpreneur?

If your reading this book, chances are you've already determined you qualify as a Careerpreneur. You may have never heard the term before but after reading the description of "what's inside" this book, something peaked your interest and made you say, "Hey, I think that's me"... right? Well join the club. I had never heard the term Careerpreneur, didn't know it pre-existed the dream I had about this umbrella term until a TP team member and very near and dear friend said during a Google+ hangout meeting "hey, have you googled that yet?" The thought never crossed my mind! All I knew is that I had dreamt up the word and the definition, which was undoubtedly going to be the same as what I'd find if the word pre-existed my dream. Whelp, that's not at all what I found. Although there were two awesome women who wrote books with the word Careerpreneur in the title, they both defined them similarly to one another though very different from what I deem it means. To them, Careerpreneurs are those who want to simply make careers out of entrepreneurship. As you know, the definition I lead with has a completely different connotation.

If you are an awesome woman or fearless man who has experienced the following- then you fit the bill:

> Have you invested years of time, money and energy into education related to a specific profession or your climb up the corporate ladder?
>
> Do you have a good reputation in your chosen profession?

Have you established hundreds perhaps even tons of contacts in your time as a professional?

Are you pretty well known in your niche amongst your professional peers?

Would you say that you are dang good at what you do?

Do you like what you do but have felt unfulfilled for at least the last few years doing it?

Have you found yourself playing in the entrepreneurial sandbox in various ways over the last few years (everything from networking marketing, direct sales, *side hustle* sales that may or may not incorporate talents you have, to making a business out of babysitting or being a nanny)?

Do you have a very tangible business or business idea that you've been pondering over for years, perhaps even executed into a form that has pulled dollars in but feel like you haven't gone into full throttle launch mode yet?

And last but not least, are you someone that naturally introduces yourself to others for the first time, 9/10 times you are likely to lead with Hi, my name is…and I'm a…professional; but it never seems to include the words entrepreneur straight off the bat?

If you answered yes to at least 7 of the 9 statements above, then you are who I would define as a Careerpreneur.

Although there is nothing wrong with the other two authors definition, I just want to make it clear why you chose this book as it resonates with the definition above. You're not a typical entrepreneur who left corporate America or your professions exclaiming you hate it and you're burned out. You actually like, you may even love what you do. You've just felt incomplete. Deep down inside you always knew you were meant to do more, go to another level and help people in a way that reaches them at a level that you feel you communicate best. Some of you are medical professionals by day and aspiring global mentors by night. Others might be renowned academics building their own brick and mortar or online universities.

The point is, as a Careerpreneur, your entrepreneurial self and your professional/career ladder executive self may or may not appear to be directly linked on the surface. But to be successful, they have to speak to each other. Your ideal entrepreneurial playground must be where your skills, talents and gifts meet. The title of your company doesn't matter. It's the role you play in it that will separate you from creating a successful venture and one that was that *thing you use to do...*

What this book will do is set up basic tenants to kickstart you into high gear as a Careerpreneur. It has been written to motivate those of you who have begun to walk your road to awesome and created your best-fit business and will empower those who are preparing to launch and just need a kick in the heels to get activated. Full of tips and techniques to get you moving in the right direction, it's not meant to be a sit down novel read. Though you will find yourself referencing it as you move forward on the road of success, I will advise you once that it's in your best interest to read it through page by page prior to utilizing the tips or forms including. As a professional, you're walking along that type- **A** personality line and most likely have regurgitated a quick response thought that you are further along in the process than you truly are. I did that too! By skipping steps and rushing through, we skip the lesson that comes along with applying the step and by unintentional consequence end up with an unnecessary mess.

Warning noted. Now let's get down to business.

Chapter 1 Stages of Growth

You've moved **beyond** *dreamer* and over into the acceptance phase of your life where your **now a** *believer*. You left the denial phase when you realized that you were designed for a purpose. At last, your finally thru thrashing with the inner conflict that you are being selfish...there are so many people out there who don't have half as much as you do. They haven't amassed as many accolades, degrees, certifications, continuing education credits or even as much notoriety amongst their peers. You've gotten over the mental hump of the "how dare I syndrome," where you stressed yourself out about how you can't possibly deserve a next level when so many people around you are striving to be where you are and go where you've gone. You've accepted that you were in fact meant for greater. This doesn't mean that you are better than anyone else. It simply means that your capacity for *going thru* is deeper because your next level is higher than the one before.

So all the previous accolades aside, you are ready to straighten out your back, lift your shoulders and posture yourself to walk up the next step without looking back into the depths of doubt. Everyone in a while you will need to remind yourself that the skills you cultivated in your profession, all the time, money and energy you invested in your profession was not for naught. You are capable of taking those hard earned skills, blending them with your talents and delivering them through your gifts as you march with a steady but full throttle pace into entrepreneurship. No more self-negative talk, reminders of how you're not really new at this because talk...no wonderment of what people will think about this newly re-vamped, spotlight version of the bolder more balanced you. Breath-ing in with a deep controlled breath, three seconds to inhale and five seconds to exhale... You got this. Now it's time to set your men-tal in gear and cheer your way thru this next level of you.

Chapter 2 Picking Your POM POM's

So what are these pom pom's I've referenced thus far? Well as you will see it's part of a system that you will use to create order, provide balance and develop your boundaries through. This system is used in your life and your business. Truly **what would a successful Careerpreneur be** if he or she doesn't have those things in place? Well, wacky on the inside might be part of what you'd be without it. Now don't get me wrong. There are thousands of people who define themselves as successful that don't have balance or good boundaries. Some of them will yell from the roof tops that they've gotten to where they are by even being bold...by their definition of it. Here are another two clarification points for you before you move forward.

First, **success is not defined by your bank account**. Although you do want to be able to eat, and preferably comfortably, you have reached a true measure of success when you are doing what you love and you're not losing out on sharing or being loved in the process. You don't have to choose your family over success. You don't have to choose a success over a meaningful relationship. You definitely don't have to choose isolation from friends and family because you're successful. True success has a balanced blend of all of those things! And guess what? You get to do more, share more and love more because of it.

People who say you have to choose have simply chosen to be unbalanced. They've prioritized the wrong thing, even if they claim it was for the right reason. We've heard their stories before. Some have said it was because they never wanted to live in poverty or struggle the way their parent's had to. They wanted to give back in a meaningful way to their community. We've also heard heartfelt stories where they discussed the violence they were exposed to or succumbed because of lack of means so they made a decision at some defining point in their lives to push hard and succeed at *all cost.*

Whelp, guess what? I share all of those stories and more and I'm a walking, breathing reality that you don't have to choose to have success over all else. What you do need are your priorities in order and to integrate them in your daily life. Even when things get hard, in order to continuously triumph over the inevitable *go thru* that you will need to climb in order *to get to* your next level, you must move from **dreamer**....**believer**...in to a **planner** that becomes an ultimate **doer**. Pom Pom's are simply an acronym for the part of the system you need to succeed as a Careerpreneur. It stands for Prioritize, organize and manage. Then you repeat! This is why we say POM POM's. We don't want you to forget the essential process of repetition.

Second, the very people who walk around claiming they are big and bold and it's what got them to the level of success they are in, typically define it incorrectly. Those folks express their boldness by saying anything and everything out of their mouths, pretty much whenever they want. Not quite how I define it and definitely not the way I would suggest a Careerpreneur live it. **Being bold means being humble**. Hmm, what did you say Naketa? Aren't those two different points on the continuum of thought? Nope! The reason you sat back, raised your eye brow and huffed at that point is probably because you consider the definition of humility to be passive, devoid of emotion and simply closed mouthed. Well maybe YOU don't think that....but you've heard other people reference it that way right? Humility is being strong enough in mind and character to know when and when not to say something. In order to be bold, you have to be humble. Boldness is merely the expression of humility. **You don't crush someone's spirit just because you can**. You definitely don't embarrass someone (even if they seem to deserve it) simply because you want to show others that you are a wordsmith and can really "read" this person up and down.

Chapter 2 Picking Your POM POM's

I'm a huge believer in never pulling out cards you don't have to until…well you have to. I don't walk in to a family function wearing my I have a triple major, masters, working on my doctorate and I'm an expert hat. If family and friends are debating on a local news conflict concerning something in one of my expertise areas, I'm not going to jump in and say "hey hey hey, wait a minute now…I'm the expert here…eh he…let me weigh in and set you guys straight."

No, I listen in perhaps ask a few questions to gain a better understanding of why they are thinking along the continuum of thought they are on and unless they are saying something that could hurt someone if they're not shown the other side of that continuum I leave it be. I take the stance that I will of course never allow a friend, family member or foe to intentionally embarrass themselves in the public domain on an area that I can lend clarity on. However, I'm also not going to walk around like misses know it all because I happen to know a lot. A consummate professional who's quite achieved and lives a fulfilling life I am. Someone who knows everything and can speak to every experience I am not. This is where I nudged into that self-reflective moment of making sure you **know thy self** if you want to truly walk in boldness and build a successful legacy.

Chapter 3 First Fruits Prioritization

This is the area you dedicate to yourself to build your mind, body and spirit. You may decide to limit this area to 15 minutes in the morning, squeeze in another 20 minutes in the afternoon and weight the heaviest portion to the evening; vice versa or somewhere muddled throughout the day. The important thing to note here is that it must be done! You have to come first in order to have energy for what needs to get done.

An example of what First Fruits Prioritization looks like for me on a typical day-

6:00am {**Feeding My Spirit**} Devotionals (Prayer, Study, Reflections & Praise)

6:50am {**Strengthening My Body**} Spinning

7:ooam {**Fine tuning My Mind**} After my spin warm up before I go into a speed session, I listen to an audio book, professional development tele-course or rehearse for an upcoming speech

7:30am/7:50am {**Fortifying My Family**} On a non-school day, I'm able to start breakfast, my daughter's hair or some other level of family focused dedicated time and get them together and off to camp, work etc. before heading into my day. Of course if this is a school day- my whole program shifts up about an hour- making Devotional time around 5am.

Chapter 4 General Office Hours

It's important to have office hours no matter where your office is located. This not only helps others to respect your time, knowing when the best time to connect with you about your organizational affairs; it helps your mind to understand when it's time to **switch on** your focused self and take you out of First Fruits mode or pull you away from Saving the World mode...

Office Hours should be spent doing the following:

Check voicemails

Check emails

Writing out- in order of priority- who needs a call back/email response TODAY

Putting all others into your Follow-up System with a calendar reminder to do so...

Following up with those who are now due for a Follow-up (*see section on Harvest Time*)

Providing client services if applicable

Managing Client service department if applicable

Building Relationships (*see next session*)

Managing your team if applicable or the systems necessary to maintain organizational balance (fiscal responsibilities/budgeting/vendor relations etc.)

Prospect Outreach

Writing Proposals

Solidifying Contracts

Implementing Marketing Strategy (*developed during Lab time*)

A typical office hour is 10am-4:30pm Tuesday-Thursday. Of course, exceptions are made if I have a networking event, prospect meeting or private coaching session that may fall outside of these hours. Nonetheless, I try to spend the majority of "live time" where I am accessible during these hours.

Chapter 5 Specialized Office Hours

This is time that is also within your "office hours" that you are NOT accessible. Meaning, that unless there is some equivalent to a fire, profuse bleeding or broken bones around you, the goal is to focus and zone in on designing, developing or refining products that accentuate your business. This is your Working ON your business time, whereas general office hours are for Working IN your business. Does that make sense?

I dedicate at least 1-2 full days per week for Lab Time. Typically, Monday's and Fridays are reserved for that special Off-limits time. Now this doesn't mean that if you have an opportunity to meet with a high-end prospect, a client that you are already servicing has a special one-time need for flexibility or you are invited to a forum/conference/event where you could grow your business that you say, "Oh no, that's my off-limits time," and miss out! As Careerpreneurs, we have to be strategically agile. In other words, be deliberate, calculative and flexible!

What this does mean is that you don't use your Lab time, whether it is a few carved out hours or dedicated days to become the catchall for everything and everyone else! Boundaries are important and without them, you're liable to loosing important ON time in your business and be stuck working IN your business for many more moons than you'd prefer.

Lab time should be where you handle the following:

Industry research

Developing Marketing Strategy

Creating or Refining Marketing Design (aspect of your Branding!)

Create new products or services

Write or update curriculums, content for your books, blogs, newsletters, warm letters, etc.

Tighten your funnel (we will discuss more about this later)

Write out thank you notes to current clients (believe it or not you will find that doing this turns into a bit of a muse for new or up-graded product and service ideas that can go into the "to be con-tinued jar...")

Pre-record webinars, create information based video's and/or podcast that explain what you do and how your services can benefit your target market

Notably, as you grow- so shall your team and many of the things listed under General and Special Office time will be removed from your list. You will see the shift of responsibilities disappear from the IN to ON side of your business. This is a key sign of productive growth. Remember you didn't get into business to work in a bubble. You want to stimulate the economy that your business is fed off by providing jobs to others, sharing your knowledge and creating the balanced life you've envisioned for your family. You know that 6-8/hr day – Three day work week you've been plotting on...

Chapter 6 Relationship Management

This is not a linear process and will be scattered throughout your day and week. To be completely honest, this is the one area that needs to be integrated into nearly every day you're in the office (general and special office hours). Relationship Management involves the connecting and engagement process.

Here you will include:

Time for formal networking

- BNI groups

- Chamber groups/events

- Urban League

- Industry specific meetings

- Private Membership Groups that maybe exclusive to you by gender, professional career or license, alumni based, etc.

Time for informal networking

- Social Events where you know your target market may hang out

  - Golf clubs

  - Tennis clubs

  - Country clubs/Spas

High Teas

Social Media Management

> Posting Value Rich content on platforms where your target market is engaging
>
> > Instagram
> >
> > Pinterest
> >
> > Facebook
> >
> > LinkedIn
> >
> > Twitter
> >
> > Tumbler
> >
> > Youtube
> >
> > Google +
> >
> > Blogger/Wordpress
>
> Commenting on post
>
> Replying to your post
>
> Posting questions/surveys/polls that increase engagement
>
> Joining and engaging in social media groups

Taking photos and posting relatable information that your market would find interesting and comment worthy

Joining Boards/Committees relevant to your Industry

This is a great way to get involve and build relationships with industry peers

*Be mindful not to OVERCOMMIT yourself and only join or participate in things where you will be a valuable asset and your time will be respected.

The key to relationship management is your consistency. No one is going to want to become your business playmate and build a rela-tionship with you if the next time they turn around you just stop meeting them at the sandbox. That doesn't mean you can't put feel-ers out, check out the scenery and research where you want to play, however you want to be clear in your introduction that it's your first time visiting and you are trying to learn more about that forum. You can spell that out in virtual and real time introductions so people know how to handle you. Some will be more or less hesitant to em-brace you based on that transparent introduction. Nonetheless it's necessary and helps you understand the power of Attracting by re-pelling (we'll talk more about this down the road).

Chapter 7 Harvest Time

When you go to the aforementioned places to connect and engage, you should approach people with one primary question and three baskets in mind. The question you lead with is what determines if their fruit is ripe to pick.

The baskets are where you will place them in your mind and in your follow-up system, which will dictate what type of follow-up you do.

Your fruit choosing question is, "How can I help you?" Based on that answer and a bit of conversational engagement, you will decide if you will put them in one of these baskets:

Referral Source: Someone who may work with or come in contact with potential prospective clients **and** who genuinely seems interested in learning more about what you do at a later time.

Prospect: Someone who fits your target client specs to the T, which means they want and could benefit from your service. What's missing is the know-like-trust factor that will take time as you build a relationship with them that displays your value and credibility. All converted clients should of course turn into a referral source as they receive quality services!

Resource: Someone who offers complimentary or even competitive services or products that your clients could benefit from. This is a tough area for people to digest, however it's covered in detail in the Careerpreeneurs Survival Suite 6-week program and for Private

Clients who are in the Harvest Time Stage of their goal development.

Remember the fortune is in the follow-up. If you aren't making time to follow-up on those people you are spending time connecting and engaging with, then ultimately you can't convert them into ripe fruit for one of your baskets. Not to be coy here, but the fruit is your fuel for your business. Money Matters! So you have to either be referred to people who want to purchase your product/service, be actively selling to clients and finding new ways to stay competitive in the market by offering your current clients and prospects the best value for their dollar so you become the go-to for your industry.

Undoubtedly, you have to make time for this and it has to be a priority! The best way to do that is to carve out a specific time during your office hours that's dedicated just for this cause. I encourage all private clients to assess what their peak *Take Over the World* time of day is, where their brain, attention to detail and energy is at its best and dedicate time within that range to schedule those 1:1 follow-up meetings, conference calls and virtual appointments with those ripe fruit connections.

Chapter 8 Designer Tassels

The next two chapters are focused on providing you with an array of tangible tips to design the tassels that make your pom pom's sparkle. Overtime, with more experience, walking the path of your *go thru* and once you are connected to aligned minds; you will add more tassels and gain custom ways to order your steps in a way that fits your personal and professional Careerpreneur-self best.

Remember, sometimes you have to be your own cheerleader! This doesn't make you more or less feminine. It's just a cold hard fact. Though supports are always encouraged and relationships should be built and maintained, there will be times when you are left alone to motivate yourself through some sticky moments and as always, you will need to hold yourself accountable for the success you build or choose not to.

Broken down into digestible bites of life, business and core tips, the advice in this section has been created for you to apply where you feel it's best applicable.

> **Life Tips** are generally applied in preparation for and throughout the First Fruits Prioritization are of your day
>
> **Business Tips** are best applied during your General and Specialized Office Hours
>
> **Core Tips** are those that are integrated in the way you think and should become a part of your mental processes as they

help your subconscious discernment muscle and develop strategic methodologies. They are best applied during your Relationship Management and Harvest Time areas

As a quick key, the labels besides each tip are a guideline for where to apply. So, if you see a tip under business that you can or should use in your personal life, please use your discretion and feel free to do so. Nearly all tips could go in the *core* category but that wouldn't make for an easily digestible meal if we gave it one gigantic whole melon would it?

Chapter 9 Spark It Up!

Well what are you waiting for? It's time to design your pom pom's.

Life Tips

Many of us don't understand the impact that balance, or the lack thereof can have on your personal and professional life. It's imperative that we weigh our time according to what produces the most significant outcomes if we want to see short term progress and lasting long term results.

Infusing Balance: For you to infuse balance into your life, it's important to establish your vision so you are clear on where you are going (personally and professionally). Your vision is the first ingredient in your batter of success and is in itself the purposeful plan of your company. Your vision must answer the question of what imprint you or it will leave on this world and the value you will bring to it."

Feel like you're walking in two worlds? Grab a dry erase board, preferably 24x36 or larger and put it on a wall that you walk by daily, at home or in your office. Write out your personal vision at the top with a bold marker and leave space for your mission statement. Make sure to stop by the visual of your vision every single day and read it out loud in your most serious and passionate voice. Rehearsing this back to yourself daily will be a conscious reminder to your subconscious of your purpose and pathway that will center you in your daily walk. Sometimes we all need reminders of where we are going so we can stay grounded when the world seems to pull us in polar opposite directions. Stay true to yourself and speak what you seek.

Chapter 9 Spark It Up!

Pencil yourself in for at least twice per week and take 30-45 minutes for Claritude! Yes, that is a made up word. It's the time you will need to gain clarity and give gratitude for all that has already been done and the achievements you've made. Taking time out for your own personal My I Need To (M.I.N.T) moments are imperative for your mental health and will lead to increases in work productivity. Remember to put the oxygen mask on yourself so you have energy, time and breath left to aide others...

In order to increase your time management skills you can't be afraid to get dirty! At TP we call this dirt exactly what it is...m.u.d- which stands for **m**anaging **u**navoidable **d**elays. Successful time managers know that you can't plan for every interruption, distraction or delay; but you sure can be proactive by imbedding a little " just in case I need to wash up again to get the mud off" into every major time slot. This translates into, cushion for those of you who can't get past the dirty reference. If you have a 6pm meeting on Tuesday evening that will take you 30 minutes to get to in light to medium traffic, then plan for 45minutes to an hour! That way you won't rush into the meeting sweaty, out of breath and scary looking because of that unavoidable traffic you hit! If anything you may be a bit early, can relax a little and build some connections before the masses rush in!

Did you know that well formulated goals have four main parts? First, they must incorporate what you want to achieve (your overall why for desiring this goal). Second, you need to be honest about where you are now in the process of attaining this goal (being at ground zero is completely okay). Thirdly, the components or tools you need to achieve that goal. Lastly, you need to create a plan for how to measure your progress toward that goal.

A sure fire way to measure your progress is to set up success indictors. Depending on your goal, indicators are the actual measuring instrument such as the number of pages or chapters completed in your book by month one, three and five... It's important to have success indicators because they keep you motivated and will serve as accountability markers when it's time to realign your priorities in order to complete your goals. – Of course this is pure example of a tip that should apply across all levels of your life, business and core....

In your relationships at home, with external family and friends, be bold.

Business Tips

Write down everything that you do to make money. If you have partners, volunteers, interns or contractors in your circle, write their name next to the things they can either assist with or handle based on their expertise. Delegate those things and make room for YOUR expertise area. Remember, everything in excellence.

If you spend 80% of your day working on the aspects of your business that increase your ROI and raise productivity, then you can spend the balance of that time strategically planning how to improve processes tomorrow. Don't get caught doing more planning than implementation. Remember the 80/20 rule applies to more than just healthy eating and junk food!

Have 5 great ideas in your head for how to share your message, impact the world and make a profit but don't know where to begin? Start with brain dumping! Yes, I said that out loud... pour your ideas into an audio recorder on your smartphone or jot them down 1990's style with a pen and piece of paper! Don't worry about grammar, format or proper pronunciation- just dump. Get those ideas out of your head and into something that can capture them in time. Once you do that, you can go through the process of filtering the dreams (thoughts with no action) from the vision (goals with a mission filled with measureable objectives).

Organize your work day in advance by creating a Filter and Flush system! 10-15 minutes per week can make a huge difference and save you hours of time! Set up folders to filter important sender based information and flush trash by unsubscribing from things you don't need once per week. Lock the filter-flush system time in your calendar so you don't get overwhelmed and spend valuable hours wasting away...

Technology for Business: Technology moves fast! Every week, there's a new invention on the market – a must have for the ever-growing number of techies. It is important for business owners to keep an eye on the many new gadgets hitting the marketplace. We've seen the smart phone and tablet become an integral part of today's daily business operations. Don't allow yourself to become overwhelmed by the options and bells and whistles of today's gadgetry. Invest some time into learning what technology might work best for your company. Stop by a local electronics store and engage the nearest techy in what's new and what devices might best serve your purposes. Who knows... in addition to accelerating your business with some new equipment, maybe you can soon count yourself among the new and proud techies.

Did you just realize how powerful social media platforms like LinkedIn, Facebook, Twitter and Pinterest can be for your professional status and business? If you're a relationship manager like me, then you probably didn't give it the credence that it deserved because you pride yourself on those 1:1 interactions right? Well that being said, I have news for you- there is value in it if you use it right! First off- you have to ask your peers, colleagues, customers and clients who send you all of those glorifying comments via email and in-person to log into social media and literally put you on blasts! Don't be shy, be bold. Recommendations and referrals are the life blood of your business and it's how employers are literally "comparison shopping" for candidates. Make sure you're at the top of mind for onlookers!

The best mini tip in the world: Only Flag or Star task that need to be followed-up on! Otherwise your email looks like a bad mockup of the battle of Germantown. You don't have to flag a good read, just set a custom reminder to come back to that during an expected information break. Flags, Stars and other "red" prompts truly should be reserved for important follow-ups.

Set a time at the top and bottom of the day to check voicemails. By utilizing this sandwich approach, you are able to begin your day with a clear understanding of what fires or emergencies need to be put out and you end your day with a window path of clarity for how to set up your tomorrow!

Consider Priority management software like Asana; Mavenlink; Basecamp; Zoho or Podio to organize yourself and your team. One of the best reasons to use this software is it limits the overflow of project and task related emails and categorizes them in a succinct pod! This makes accountability and accountability checks a breeze.

Chapter 9 Spark It Up!   25

When you write your "get it done list", group similar task together. For example, return phone calls, email replies or compilations should be completed in one sitting. Ideally, you will have a higher success rate if you return calls at 15 minutes after the hour, as most people schedule there appointments on the hour. This little tidbit has worked for me over 15 years!

If you are an aspiring author, speaker or trainer- make sure you set the scales in your favor before launching yourself on full throttle mode! Engage with your respective audience through informative blogs, creative whitepapers and participate in interviews. Don't be afraid to contact your local chamber of commerce or non-profit organization and give them a 30 minute taste of your skills! Remember that you have invested in yourself; you value your work and have tons to offer. Don't keep all of that goodness to yourself!

As you develop your business, see progress and experience failures, it will be easy to fall into a pit of self-wallowing that lends you to tilt the scales of time too much on either the office hour or home end depending on your mental state. Although some days will call you to carry a heavier load then others, it will be important to level out your average with fair equilibrium. Remember to work hard at creating balance.

Core Tips

Did you know great leaders know how to follow? Well good. Now I need you to understand that great leaders also know how to model their leadership through their actions and not their words. It's not enough to tell people how to do/where to go/or how to behave. It's not even enough to follow someone else and let them take the lead every once in a while. Your supporters are often supported because they are encouraged by what they *see* you do. If you find yourself under pressure, feeling overwhelmed and constrained by projects without enough time to do them, how you handle those situations will determine how your supporters handle theirs.

Are you looking for a mentor? Before you go out making calls and searching the top ranks for industry leaders for your mentor-match, you have to put in a little work on the back end so you can see results on the front. First, know what you want! Write out a short list of very clear and specific goals that you would like your mentor to guide you through and be clear about your expectations. Second, do your due diligence! Conduct a needs assessment via a SWOT analysis (Strengths/Weaknesses/Opportunities/Threats) on yourself (whatever that primary mentorship objective is) and be prepared to work on strengthening your weak and threat areas before working with a mentor. Once you've done those things, and you have a few successful people in mind- you must prepare yourself to become acquainted with his or her work! Read their books, articles and blogs. Chat with them on twitter or Facebook and show your worth! Mentorship is a lot of time and commitment on both ends so you have to be willing to demonstrate yours! At the end of the day, there is no loss for you if that person doesn't want to take on the task of guidance in that moment. You've been building yourself up the whole time right? Remember that your purpose is not based on someone else's yes or no, however their success isn't built around making time for someone who isn't willing to invest in themselves either...Preparation is key.

The best way to Know Your Lane is to understand what direction you're going in. Write out the top 3 things you want to achieve and then create a path to get there. Sounds simple but as your aware it's not. One of the main reasons this feels harder than it has to be, is because we often forget to analyze ourselves in the process. It's important to understand your limitations as a driver before you venture out on a 3 day-driving trip right? Do you need to stop every 2hrs to stretch, can you drive well in the rain, and do long stretches of highway bother your eyes? All important questions that the answers to help prepare you for a less stressful adventure. This same simple Q & A is necessary in your business! Ask yourself what you like, don't like, what are you good at, what are you great at and what you love.

Looking for love in all the wrong places? Does anyone else remember that song besides me? Well today it's more than a quotable from our past that we can sing out loud as we make fun of our previous choices. It applies to what we do to ourselves personally and professionally. We are often so busy seeking and searching the answers that we often miss the solutions. If you are concerned that you are on the wrong path in your business or as you re-establish your brand, consider that you are looking in the wrong places for the right answers! Stop trying to work in a bubble or surrounding yourselves with YES people who aren't taking YOU seriously enough to tell you the truth! If you know you need a personal or professional assessment but you know your time and money is short, consider virtual programs that you can work on at your own pace until you're ready for something more intensive like Balance Beam. The point is to do something strategically created to move you forward in the RIGHT direction.

Managing relationships is never easy. Whether they are personal or professional, because you are dealing with people (note you are one as well), there are likely to be misunderstandings, assumptions or perceptions that ensue a conflict that will need expedient resolution. A way to minimize these fires and prevent some altogether is to develop boundaries from the offset. Boundaries are there to provide clarity and avoid the *if only's*. You know, the statements that come after the fire has gotten out of control… "*If only I had known you wouldn't appreciate that, If only you had told me you don't like when I say things like that…*" Minimize the conflict inside you and for others by forming better boundaries.

Appendix I: POM POM Complete

POM POM

Prioritize Organize Manage

Repeat

Prioritize Organize Manage

Complete

First Fruits Prioritization:

General Office Hours:

Special Off-limits Office Hours-Lab Time:

Relationship Management:

Harvest Time:

Appendix II: POM POM Mind Map

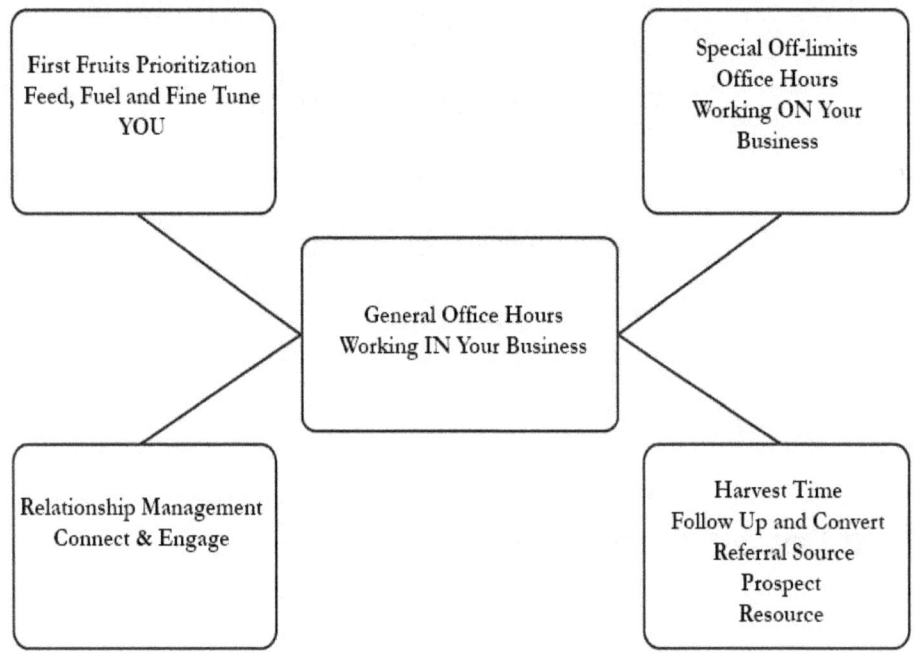

About The Author

Naketa R. Thigpen, MSS, LCSW
Advisor to Advisors

Naketa Thigpen is a challenger, one whose clear purpose is to task others to greatness. As the President and co-founder of Thigpro, a life management and professional development company, her inimitable ability to develop the person inside the professional through customized programs and simplistic systems is precisely what makes her the premier specialist in coaching. As an Advisor to Advisors, she designs tools, like her proprietary **Permission to Pause** Corporate and Community Events that help corporate leaders and creative entrepreneurs build efficient work-structures that allow them to effectively infuse balance into their life and business. Naketa is a motivation maven, Empowerment Speaker and Author who has published several books including Leadership Essentials Kit for the Busy Be, Barrier Breakers Reference Guide & Workbook, Leading A Balanced Life: A Workbook for Time Limited Professionals, and Careerpreneurs Kickstart: 25 Ways to Subtract Fear and Add Success to Your Business.

As a Licensed Clinical Social Worker with expertise in Relationship Management, Trauma and related Behavioral modalities, Naketa Thigpen realized that she could impact the world in a unique way by integrating her skills, gifts and talents as a holistically centered success coach. A candidate at Walden University, Public Health-Community Health Education/Corporate Wellness & Employee Retention, graduate of Bryn Mawr College Graduate School of Social Work and Social Research and obtained her Bachelors of Science degree in Psychology, Sociology, and Anthropology from Drexel University.

In designing real solutions to real problems that exist within the business and personal worlds of today's leaders, Naketa is determined to move them beyond excellence and into the rare air of greatness system implementation, innovative mindset modificationandbalance.

To introduce yourself to Naketa, email her your business, leadership or mindset related question to asknaketa@thigpro.com . Your question could be featured on the next episode of Balance Beam on ThigProMedia TV.

About The Company

Thigpen's Professionals, LLC is a Life Management Consulting and Professional Development Services Company that takes a synergistic approach to infusing work-life balance in business.

For the last 3 years, the family owned company has invested in sustainability. We want to provide opportunities for personal and professional growth in order to build stronger families and enhance the overall social health of our global community members. Our organization focuses on the unique needs of the individuals and organizations that we serve. The Life Management Consulting services are offered through our Permission to Release Your Success programs, designed to help professional women who are entrepreneurs achieve growth by learning how to establish health boundaries, achieve work-life balance through strategic planning and put their strategies to action through calculated bold steps. Thigpro, our Professional Development Services division is tailored to organizations who seek to enhance communication within and between executive tiers and improve organizational synergy which will increase their Return on Investment (ROI).

If you are not already a part of our thriving community of Kickstarters-Join the Revolution of Creatives and Business Leaders who want to 10xtheirFocus!

To receive Insider tips on kickstarting your focus to get ahead in life and business, gain the latest news to infuse for strategic tools you can use in your daily life- visit us at www.thigpro.com/community

www.ingramcontent.com/pod-product-compliance
Lightning Source LLC
Chambersburg PA
CBHW070723180526
45167CB00004B/1587